W9-BUF-014

22.95

Crusader Castles

Christian Fortresses in the Middle East

Brian Hoggard

rosen central™

Published in 2004 by The Rosen Publishing Group, Inc.
29 East 21st Street, New York, NY 10010

First Edition

Library of Congress Cataloging-in-Publication Data

Hoggard, Brian.
Crusader castles: Christian fortresses in the Middle East/
by Brian Hoggard.
    p. cm.—(The library of the Middle Ages)
Includes bibliographical references and index.
ISBN 0-8239-4212-0 (lib. bdg.)
1. Fortification—Middle East—History—Juvenile literature.
2. Crusades—Juvenile literature. 3. Castles—Middle East—
History—Juvenile literature. 4. Architecture, Medieval—Middle
East—History—Juvenile literature. 5. Military architecture—
Middle East—History—Juvenile literature.
I. Title. II. Series.
UG432.M628H64 2003
909.07—dc21

                                                    2003001915

Manufactured in the United States of America

Table of Contents

An aerial view of Kyrenia Castle on the north coast of Cyprus, an island used by the crusaders as a staging area for their invasions of the Holy Land

The Castle Builders

n the eastern edge of the Mediterranean Sea, there is an area known to people throughout the world as the Holy Land. Today we know the main part of this area as Israel, and its main city is Jerusalem. The Holy Land is the place where Jesus was born and died, and where many other events described in the Bible took place. It is because of this that the area is very sacred to Christians. But this is a sacred place for Muslims and Jews, also, who have many important religious reasons for being in this place. All of these people with different religions want to be able to visit this area to pray, and because of this there have been lots of arguments, stretching far back into history, over who owns the Holy Land.

In AD 1095, Christians in western Europe decided that they wanted to control the Holy Land and own the places that were important in Jesus' life. So they set off on the first of many Crusades to fight the Muslims who were living there so that they could have the land for themselves. Christian armies came from France, Germany, and many other parts of Europe, but because most of them spoke French, the Muslims called these first crusaders Franks. Many big battles took place and many people died in this struggle. The Muslims fought back courageously, so it took a long time for the crusaders to succeed in their goal. In 1099, they finally conquered Jerusalem and achieved effective control of the Holy Land. They slaughtered the Muslim population of the city they conquered, along with many Christians and Jews who got in the way. To keep control of the place, the crusaders had to build castles to stop the Muslims from winning back the land. Manpower was always a problem for the crusaders in the Middle East, and it was thought that well-built stone fortresses would compensate the crusaders for their disadvantage in numbers. Some of these castles were very big, even compared to the biggest ones in Europe. Without them the crusaders would not have been able to keep their new conquests out of the hands of the Muslims, who represented a continuous threat along the borders of their new Christian states.

It was very difficult for the Christians to control the Holy Land because Muslims and other people kept trying to invade and reconquer it. To keep control, the crusaders often had to ask for help from western Europe, so more crusaders would be sent to fight off the latest invasions. Since all of these fierce knights and soldiers needed castles from which to fight, the whole time the crusaders were in the Holy Land new castles were often built and old castles were made stronger. Over the two centuries that the crusaders held the Holy Land, the castles and fortifications that were created, adapted, and maintained by them were

Knights in hand-to-hand combat, from a twelfth-century German illuminated manuscript

the only reason that they were able to stay there at all. In this book, the creation of these castles and the way they were used will be explored.

The Crusades began with a speech made by Pope Urban III in 1095 at Clermont in France, where he beseeched the rulers of the West to reclaim the Holy Land for Christianity. In his speech, the pope promised people that they would be forgiven for their sins if they took part in the Crusade, as an incentive to make them go. Many people had been taught by the Church that they would go to hell when they died, so taking part in the Crusade must have seemed like a good opportunity to find spiritual peace and eternal salvation. For many people, the prospect of making money out of conquering another country was also appealing. Some of them might be given new lands and titles while on the Crusade.

The pope also wanted to rescue the Byzantine Empire, the eastern Christian community centered around the city of Byzantium, whose leader had appealed for aid against threatening Turkish armies. Others, like the Venetians and the Genoese, who would provide transport to the crusaders across the Mediterranean Sea, looked upon the venture mainly as a way to get rich.

The response to the pope's speech was enthusiastic, and by 1099 Jerusalem had been taken. The First Crusade was a success. Four separate Christian kingdoms were established to reward the leaders of the Crusade. In order for the crusaders to keep this area under western Christian control, it was important that lords and nobles be given land there so they had material reasons to stay. In medieval Europe, under the law of primogeniture, the eldest son would inherit all the lands of his father. Younger sons had to leave their estates and seek their fortunes elsewhere, so the Crusades were a real opportunity for them to acquire their own lands, if the Holy Land could be held. As soon as the land was divided up among the crusaders, the process of securing and settling the land began and castle building began.

The castles of the Holy Land were built by three main groups of people. Each of these groups built their castles in

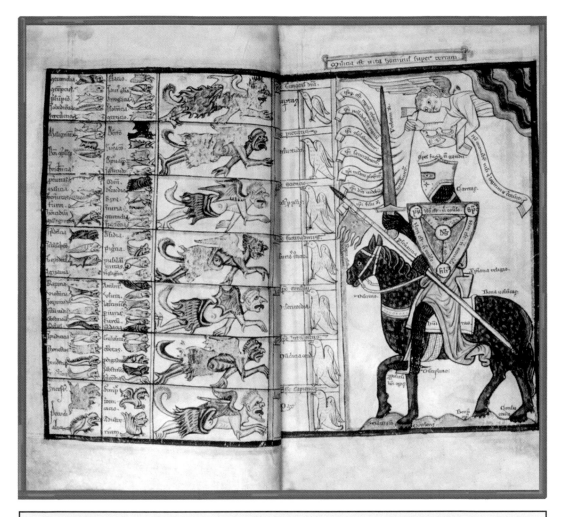

This thirteenth-century manuscript illustration depicts a knight as a Christian warrior fighting vice and heresy in the form of devils.

different ways and for slightly different reasons. The three groups who built the crusader castles were the new kings of Jerusalem, the lords and knights who took part in the Crusades, and the military orders (the warrior-monks), such as the Knights Templar and the Knights Hospitaller. Though they built castles for different reasons, they all had one thing in common: They wanted to stay in the Holy Land and keep their enemies out. The Muslims from the surrounding area and the Byzantines in earlier times had already built some castles, but many of these were damaged by the crusaders during their conquest. Thus new ones needed to be built, and older buildings were changed to be more like the type of castles that were constructed in western Europe. The crusaders knew that they had managed to conquer the castles that already existed in the area and that the Muslims were a formidable force who might do the same, so it was important to build more castles than there had been before and to make them very strong.

It was the responsibility of the king of Jerusalem to ensure the security of the new state and to decide where to build new castles. The original leader of the First Crusade was a man called Godfrey de Bouillon. His brother became the first king of Jerusalem, Baldwin I, and together they began the process of fortifying the new kingdom.

An example of an older building that was reused by the Christians was the Tower of David in the city of Jerusalem. It was an old but very strong tower and was used as one of the main defenses for the city. This tower became an important symbol for the newly conquered city and appeared on the royal seal. It wasn't until 1170, however, that its role as a military building was expanded and a palace was built next to it, all of which was then heavily fortified with ditches and walls.

A castle tower served several purposes. First of all, it gave the defenders an excellent view of the surrounding terrain and the movements of besieging armies. It provided high ground from which to shoot down on the enemy. And

An aerial view of Montreal Castle at Shaubak, Jordan. The castle was built on a hilltop to command a view of the surrounding trade routes.

if built on a corner outward from the castle walls, it enabled defenders to fire into the flanks of troops assaulting the walls.

One of the first really big new castles was called Montreal. Work on it began in 1115. This castle was built on a hill with natural defenses all around. It was common to design castles to take advantage of local terrain. One of the reasons this castle was built was so that the king could control taxes on an important trade route that ran near the site. This castle demonstrates that the

An interior view of the ruins of Montreal Castle. Construction started in AD 1115. It was one of the first truly large crusader castles.

rulers were very concerned with making sure they had money coming in from taxes at the same time that they were making sure the kingdom was safe from attack.

The importance of controlling trade routes across the Holy Land as a means of raising money cannot be overemphasized. Caravans had plied the overland trade routes across the Middle East and Asia Minor as far back as the time of the Greek city-states, several hundred years before the birth of Christ. They connected Europe to the distant and mysterious regions of China, India, and Southeast Asia, and the goods that were exchanged were very profitable. It was during the Crusades that many European nobles were first exposed to these commodities. They were thoroughly seduced by the spices, silks, porcelain, and other goods that came from the East, and their desire to control and exploit this trade was an enormous factor in the decision to join the Crusades.

The lords and knights tended to build small towers that were then intended to become the centers of large estates. They would choose an area that they thought they might like to own or live in, and then they would select the best place within that area for their tower. Usually these stone towers had a ground floor and an upper floor, and they were successful as small fortress towers. Most of them stood alone, but some of them became the center for other buildings and courtyards that were arranged around them. These castle towers could vary from thirty square feet to nearly three times that size. It wasn't just the lords and knights who built these castle towers, however. Many towers were attached to church buildings and monasteries, too. For example, it is reported that a tower was built at the Church of the Nativity in Bethlehem, and a nunnery built near Jerusalem was attached to a strong tower.

The best attempt so far at counting these small tower castles has shown that there were at least seventy-five of them and probably a good many more that we don't know about. Inside each of these towers would be a small fighting unit whose job it was to defend the surrounding lands. The large number of these small castles must have provided excellent security for the new kingdom, in addition to the much larger castles built by royalty.

The monastic military orders of the Knights Templar and Knights Hospitaller had different reasons for building castles. Both of them were charitable orders with military training whose job it was to protect Christian pilgrims who traveled to the Holy Land. The Knights Hospitaller provided accommodation for pilgrims as well as care and protection, and the Knights Templar policed the pilgrimage routes to protect pilgrims from bandits and any enemy forces in the area. The castles of the Knights Templar were, therefore, situated mostly along major roads where they could easily watch over the routes of the pilgrims. The castles of the Knights Hospitaller were usually built in more remote areas away from major roads, and, a bit like the castles of the knights and lords, formed the center of large estates, which the Hospitallers ruled.

The Templars had their headquarters very close to the Dome of the Rock in Jerusalem, which they knew as the Temple of the Lord. From here they took their name.

The gravestone of a Knight Templar with a sword and a shield bearing a cross. The Knights Templar were a religious order of monks with military training.

Castles held by the Templars included Castrum Arnaldi, Le Toron des Chevaliers, La Féve (one of their most important castles), and Maldoim. They also had many small towers in strategic places, all designed and located with the protection of pilgrimage routes in mind. The Hospitallers also had many castles, including Belmont, Belvoir, and Calansue.

The castles of these orders of knights were often designed with walled enclosures that had a passageway running around the inside of the walls. The passageway was normally covered by a roof, and there was usually a square tower at one end of the building. These castles were bigger than the towers of the lords and knights, and they provided good bases from which the knights could ride out to defend their territories when necessary. It is easy to see how this diverse range of castles would have presented a very formidable defensive network in the Holy Land.

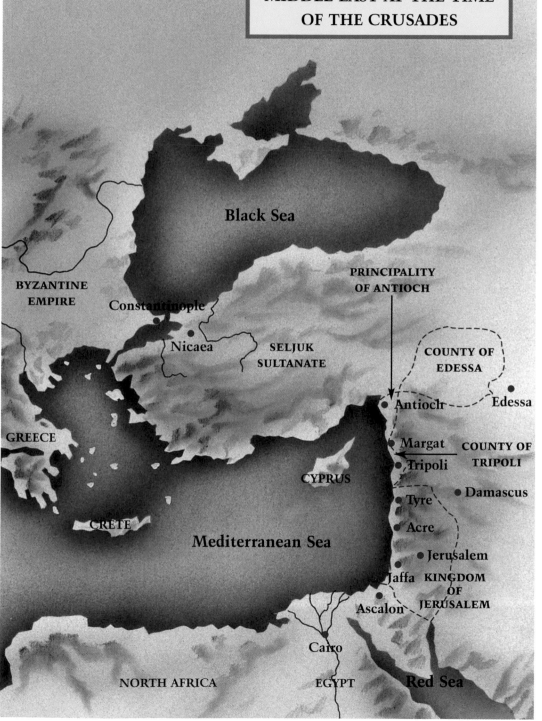

ASIA MINOR AND THE
MIDDLE EAST AT THE TIME
OF THE CRUSADES

Black Sea

BYZANTINE
EMPIRE

Constantinople

Nicaea

SELJUK
SULTANATE

PRINCIPALITY
OF ANTIOCH

COUNTY OF
EDESSA

Antioch

Edessa

GREECE

Margat

COUNTY OF
TRIPOLI

Tripoli

CYPRUS

Damascus

Tyre

CRETE

Acre

Mediterranean Sea

Jerusalem

Jaffa

KINGDOM
OF
JERUSALEM

Ascalon

Cairo

NORTH AFRICA

EGYPT

Red Sea

The embarkation of the king of France for the Holy Land during the Second Crusade of AD 1147 to 1149, from a fifteenth-century French illuminated manuscript

Building the Castles

 he construction of a castle was a serious and dangerous business, especially in a recently conquered area where the possibility of counterattack always existed. For some of the builders and stonemasons who worked on these new fortifications, it must also have seemed very hot compared to the climate back in Europe. Wherever the builders came from, the methods of constructing a castle were the same. The effort that went into building a castle and the designs of different kinds of castle will be explored here. The plans of three different castles will be examined to reveal the differences and similarities.

It is clear from records of castle building that these projects involved a large number of laborers and craftsmen and that it was a very expensive process. The construction of one castle could cost as much as a tenth of the king's annual income in one year. Annual expenditure on maintenance and repair of royal castles would amount to another tenth of his income. This is why the kings of Jerusalem wanted to secure trade routes and levy taxes as part of their military conquest of the region.

Crusader Castles

Local people were hired as laborers in the building of the castle. Work on one sizable castle could employ several thousand people over the course of its construction. A wide variety of people with different skills were involved at every stage. Reginald Allen-Brown, author of *English Castles*, presents a comprehensive summary of the different trades involved from a Norman castle-building account:

> There are references to the quarry-men, rough masons who worked the stone from the quarries, and to the freemasons who fashioned it for the walls and towers; to the wood-men who cut the timber, the carters who brought it to the site, and the carpenters who then worked it for joists and floors and roofs. There are references also to the miners who cut the fosses and hacked out the cellars in the living rock; to smiths at their forges, lime workers, hodmen, watchmen and soldiers to guard the works, and to clerks who checked materials and expenditure and drew up the accounts.

There was always someone in charge of the whole process, and that was usually the master mason, who would today be known as an architect. In essence, every single process from the cutting down of trees, to the cutting of rocks from quarries, right down to the placing of a carved stone on a wall, had to have someone do it. Someone also had to feed, clothe, and look after all the workers on the site. Imagine how many meals would have been cooked and how much water would have been drunk in the heat of the Middle East.

The head from a sculpture of a crusader taken from his tomb

The entire community who lived in the area would have been harnessed to provide food and drink for the workers and craftsmen. Other supplies and building materials would be brought in from elsewhere by horse and cart. The demands of this army of workers may have overwhelmed the communities they occupied, and it is probable that everything the local people owned was taken for the castle project and their new lords. The large number of new castles and small fortifications erected in the Holy Land at this time must have caused intense upheaval in the landscape, changing its appearance and character forever. That, of course, was the plan—to make the crusader presence impossible to ignore.

One large castle built by King Baldwin I of Jerusalem in the early twelfth century was called Li Vaux Moïse. It sits on top of a rocky ridge controlling an important trade route in the area. This castle is unusual in that its gatehouse is cut out of solid rock. The soft sandstone of the area allowed the

The ruins of the moat of the crusader fortress at Urfa in the County of Edessa in southeastern Turkey

builders of this castle to create paths and stairs cut straight into the rock. This site was chosen for the obvious reason that it has steep cliffs running around it, which meant there was only one way into the castle. Here the builders were particularly clever, because they spent time smoothing the rocks all around the castle to prevent people from climbing them. At this site, the geology of the area was a major component in the success of the castle's design. If the rock had been very hard instead of soft, the carved paths and stairs may not have been possible, nor the smoothing of the rocks around the castle. The castle is a type of fortified enclosure with a few towers around it and, beyond the walls of the castle, some lookout towers.

One of the largest castles ever built was called Chastel Pelerin, south of Acre, and it was built by the Knights Templar. Built in response to the threat of a Muslim invasion along the coast, this castle was constructed quickly but on a massive scale. It was begun in 1218 and was placed on a spit of land that stretched into the sea. The spit of land was severed from the coast with a huge ditch and a large wall some eighteen feet thick and forty-eight feet high. As if this barrier weren't enough, three projecting square towers overlooked the wall and the ditch with arrow slits, presenting a fearsome prospect to any army wishing to lay siege to the building. This castle used some very large stone blocks that the Templars took from the ruins of an ancient building on the site, which had probably belonged to the Phoenicians.

Behind the wall was a complex of halls and crypts that provided accommodations and facilities for pilgrims and Templars alike, and there was also a chapel for the Templars. It is said that during a siege in 1220 the castle was defended by 4,000 people. Only a castle of the largest proportions could hold and support this many people. The castle's location was essentially in the sea, so it was possible to receive provisions by boat as well as by land. This provided additional security. During the Muslim counterattacks on the Christian fortresses during the late twelfth century under the leadership of Saladin, the Christians were able to hold onto only those coastal towns and castles that could be supplied by sea.

Crusader castles sometimes took the shape of entire walled towns. The Templars' fortified town of Tortosa, on the

The seawall of the fortified crusader city of Tortosa, near Tartus on the coast of Syria. Some of the city's walls were seventy-five feet high. The city was never taken by force.

coast of modern Syria, was an incredible feat of engineering. A section of the internal wall seventy-five feet high still survives today. Tortosa was never taken by force, but it was eventually abandoned by the Templars after the fall of Acre in 1291. The cathedral and much of the castle ruins still stand.

The crusaders and the monastic military orders built castles throughout the period of their occupation of the Holy Land, from 1099 to 1314, a period of 215 years. Over this time, the buildings ranged from small square two-story towers to extremely large castle islands such as Chastel

The donjon, or central keep, of Chastel Blanc in Safita, Syria

Pelerin. Large hilltop castles and remote cliff-hugging fortresses were all built as part of the effort to retain this area for the Christians. The ingenuity of the master masons in adapting their art to the landscape of the Middle East is a testament to their determination to bring the area under their control.

An underground passageway at Krak des Chevaliers. The staircase leads to the main courtyard, and the corridor to the left leads to storage chambers.

Life in the Castles

Medieval castles in the Holy Land were military machines and did not contain many luxury features, unlike the amazing palaces and apartment suites that were built inside many castles in later periods. The castles of the crusader period were built principally to be functional, to serve in the defense of the newly conquered land. This isn't to say that the castles were solely about war and fighting. People lived, worked, ate, and slept inside them, too. The castles were also at the center of large estates that provided money and supplies to the lord or the military order who controlled them.

Most castles and fortresses have a strong point, a place where the defenders can retreat as a last resort if all the other defenses fail. In a large castle with concentric lines of defense, this is usually a strongly constructed building at the center of the castle called the keep. The outer defense of a castle might be a cliff, a moat, or a ditch, which runs around a strong wall with towers along it. Inside this outer wall there may be another wall with yet more towers. Within that there may be the keep or some other strong tower. The keep can also be called the donjon in the study of crusader castles. At Belvoir, one of the earliest large castles in the kingdom of Jerusalem, the central building encloses a very strongly built courtyard within the main castle walls that has towers of its own on each corner and on the east side. This was in effect a castle within a castle, and it no doubt provided an extremely strong defense.

Other large castles had more elaborate or sophisticated outer defenses and interiors furnished for more comfortable living, with less emphasis on a tough core and more emphasis on a tough outer shell. Castles such as Krak des Chevaliers, a very large castle built by the Knights Hospitaller, display such a plan, with very strong defenses circling the halls, chapel, and other buildings inside it. This type of castle had been designed so that parts of the interior could be defended were they broken into. It was quite common for crusader castles to have interiors designed with crooked passageways, corridors that went nowhere, and overhead firing positions, so that the situation could become quite desperate for attackers who actually breached the entrance and entered the castle. Krak des Chevaliers also could be provisioned with food and supplies for a siege lasting as long as two years. It had its own windmill for grinding grain, and its cistern could store two million gallons of water.

Smaller castles often had only a single strong tower on the perimeter. Even smaller were the castle towers of the knights and lords that comprised a single tower with no substantial perimeter defenses. Despite their simple plan and small scale, these towers were very strong and provided an excellent high point from which to defend against attackers. If the towers were built high enough and close enough to signal to each other, they formed a network of mutually supporting forts, and perimeter defenses were not as essential.

The design of these castles and towers was always based on military necessity, but people did try to conduct their lives within them. What went on inside when there wasn't a battle, and who lived there? An adequate supply of water and food was crucial. Without enough water or food, defenders would have to surrender a besieged castle. On the other hand, if they had enough water and food, defenders could hold their position in the castle for such a long time that the enemy might give up. Enormous underground vaults were constructed so that large quantities of food could be stored. The Hospitaller castle of Margat had huge vaults like these, which were so large that they could be used to shelter hundreds of people during times of crisis. The vaults could store a five-year food supply. It is known that in some castles, live animals were kept so that fresh milk and meat would still be available during a siege. The towns of Tyre, Antioch, Caesarea, and Jerusalem used ancient Roman aqueducts to bring water into the cities. Other castles, such as Belvoir, used large cisterns fed by rain to store water. Some castles were designed to have a deep, reliable well so that the occupants would never run out of water. Many of the castles had large stables, too, and some even had special passageways that were wide enough for horses to gallop through while offering protection from arrows and other missiles.

In most of the larger castles, there would be a gatehouse, a refectory, a kitchen, a great hall, a chapel, and many other

Margat Castle in Syria, built by the Knights Hospitaller. The castle could store a food supply for its defenders that would last five years.

rooms that could be used for living quarters or storing armor, weapons, and food. In the case of the military orders, there would also be large dormitories, and the chapel might be more centrally located than in other castles.

When not at war, castles were like the government offices for the area around them, where taxes were collected, political decisions were made, and disputes were settled. The lord or military order in charge of the castle would work with the king to ensure that the security of the kingdom as a whole was maintained. They would also send to the king taxes that they had collected from the land under their control. The castle served as an administrative center for maintaining law and order in the local populations.

As well as living among the conquered Muslim population, the western Europeans who occupied the Holy Land also lived among many Christians who had been living in the area for centuries. The Christians of the area practiced a different kind of Christianity compared to the western European invaders, and their religion was kept separate from that of the newcomers. It is easy to imagine that the people of the area felt hostile toward their new rulers for a very long time. Powerful families had their wealth taken away from them, and everyone who lived there suddenly became a lower-class citizen than they had been before. For this reason, the imposition of order was an important issue, as there was some anger aimed at the crusaders from a lot of different people. Punishments were meted out at the castle.

When not at war, the castle may have accommodated the local lord and his family. If they didn't live in a separate

Another view of Krak des Chevaliers near Homs, Syria. The arched structure in the middle is an aqueduct to supply the defenders with water.

palace in one of the towns, then normally they would live in a part of the hall of the castle, separated by a curtain or partition from the rest of the hall. The hall is also where important guests would be welcomed, and it was usually the most decorated part of the building apart from the chapel. A constable, a porter, a watchman, and a chaplain would have lived in the castle all the time, too, but other knights and soldiers would be called up as the need arose. In the Holy Land, it is likely that there would always have been some

Crusader Castles

A city plan of Jerusalem in the twelfth century. Except for its capture during the First Crusade in 1099, Jerusalem remained in Muslim hands and all subsequent Crusades were a failure.

soldiers on guard, ready to act. In a castle owned by one of the military orders, all of the knights would live in the castle in special accommodations with a separate office for their leader.

In spite of the sturdiness of these castles, the principal problem for the crusaders, throughout the time they controlled parts of the Holy Land, was lack of manpower. After the conquest of Jerusalem in 1099, most crusaders returned home. On the verge of recapturing Jerusalem from Saladin in 1191 during the Third Crusade, Richard the Lionheart instead cut a deal with Saladin to permit the passage of Christian pilgrims and then left the Holy Land. He was anxious to protect his European kingdom from the predatory actions of his brother John and the king of France. Most of the crusaders were happy to rescue the holy places of their religion and receive forgiveness for their sins in the process, but the focus of their lives and fortunes remained in western Europe. The crusaders who stayed in the Holy Land were largely an odd bunch of mavericks and adventurers, clearly outsiders in a land of hostile people, and there were never enough recruits of this type to withstand the continued assaults of Muslim armies.

In 1480, Sultan Muhammad II laid siege to the island of Rhodes, home of the Order of St. John. In this fifteenth-century painting, the Knights Hospitaller prepare to defend their island.

Castles at War

A castle was a symbol of power in a newly conquered area, and it was a place from which armed forces could quickly and efficiently spread through an area to maintain control. Not only that, it was also an extremely strong building that could survive for a long time even if the knights and soldiers out in the field had been defeated. A castle meant that knights and soldiers who rode out to battle were much fresher than they would have been if they'd come from farther away. If they were forced to retreat to the castle, they had plenty of time to regain their strength for another attempt. Castles, therefore, were like a long arm of power out in the depths of the country that had been conquered, guaranteeing that there would be no rebellion or counter-attack from enemy forces.

Castles were built in such a way that they could be easily defended, and the designers tried their best to elim-inate potential areas of weakness that an attacking force could pick on. Many architectural designs were used to help the occupants of the castle fight effectively, but ulti-mately a castle was only as strong as its weakest link, and a very determined attack would usually find that weak point. The shape of arrow slits, square or round towers, battlements, the height and thickness of walls, and the depth and width of the moat or ditch were all crucial considerations.

The width of the moat determined the effective reach of the enemy's weapons and meant that the attackers had to cross it before getting to the castle, during which time they were highly vulnerable to being shot at by archers from the castle. It is harder to throw or shoot things farther and higher, so this is where the height of the walls became important. Well-designed battlements would have thick walls to protect the archers behind them, and the slits or openings in the walls had to provide a wide field of vision for the archers but only a tiny gap for the enemy to aim at. Battlements that projected outward beyond the walls were also a good idea, because the soldiers in the castles could drop things on the heads of the enemies below. Projecting towers and bastions with holes in their floors were known as machiolations.

Very thick castle walls could withstand the impact of the enormous rocks catapulted at them, and they were resistant to fire. The height of the walls also made scaling them with ladders more difficult. The castle towers were built to protrude from the walls so that the castle defenders could look sideways along the walls and enfilade, or fire into the flanks of attacking troops. This meant that there were no blind spots where defenders could not observe enemy soldiers close to the castle walls and that the defenders on the battlements did not have to lean out over them in order to see what was going on below, leaving them vulnerable to

This thirteenth-century Venetian mosaic depicts the construction of the Tower of Babel. It reveals some of the techniques used in castle building.

attack. The shape of the towers could be important, too, and round towers were thought better than square towers at resisting catapult stones. If the enemy dug underneath the corner of a square tower it could weaken it considerably, but it was more difficult to weaken a round tower. Both types of towers were used in the Holy Land.

Castles that did not have thick walls or strong towers were vulnerable to artillery. It is not quite true that stone walls were impervious to destruction before the invention of gunpowder and cannons. Even before that time, catapults like the mangonel and the trebuchet, worked by counterweights or the torsion on twisted ropes, could hurl stones weighing as much as 600 pounds a distance of 500 feet. This was a greater range than the arrows of defending archers on a castle's walls, so these catapults could be used

A plan of the fortified city of Acre on the Mediterranean coast of modern Israel. This is a woodcut made from a drawing prepared by nineteenth-century German archaeologists.

with impunity. As the designs of such catapults improved and their accuracy and rate of fire increased, the continuous pounding by such heavy stones would bring down castle walls. The crusaders themselves used the trebuchet to great effect in their siege of Acre in 1191.

The location of the castle was perhaps the most crucial thing of all. It needed to be in a place where it commanded a good view of the surrounding territory. It had to be located at a good defensive point with respect to strategic routes, not only to control those routes, but to provide passage to a relieving army. Important ports and towns needed to be protected, too, and these were not always in easy-to-defend areas. In areas that were difficult to defend, a good plan was to build as big as possible, and this was certainly what the Knights Templar did at Tortosa with their strongly fortified walled town and castle. The location, size, and sophistication of the defenses could provide an invincible bastion if used effectively. The Templar fortresses at Chastel Pelerin and at Tortosa were never conquered by the Muslims. They were abandoned eventually, however, when it became obvious that the rest of the kingdom was lost.

One of the many events that marked the reconquest of the Holy Land by the Muslims was the siege of the fortified coastal town of Tripoli in 1289. The Templar of Tyre, a person who recorded the events at the time, wrote an account of the siege:

> The sultan set up his siege-engines both great and small, he placed his wooden tower and his catapults opposite the town, then he set his sappers to mining underground and advanced past the outer fosses. The city of Tripoli had strong stone walls, but the sultan attacked it at its weakest point—the Bishop's Tower, which was very old. The siege-engines battered it until it broke to pieces. So too with the Hospitallers' Tower, which was new and strong, but which cracked apart so widely that a horse could have gone through the gap. The sultan had so many men that every embrasure had twenty Saracen archers shooting at it, so that none of our crossbowmen dared show an eye

to take aim; any who tried to shoot was struck at once;
and so the town was in a very bad state.

The other accounts of this siege tell how the occupants of the city fled to the harbor when the walls were breached. Many of them were killed on the way and the women and children were taken hostage. The city had been held by western Europeans for 185 years. The sultan destroyed the city after capturing it.

This account shows how the army of the sultan had completely surrounded the town and how he made sure that he had archers aiming at every possible place that the castle defenders would normally shoot from. While this was happening, the sultan ordered his soldiers to dig beneath the walls and towers to weaken them. The large siege engines began hurling boulders at the walls and towers until they started to break up. Then the army poured through the gaps to capture or kill the occupants and reconquer the town. In this particular case, the assault on the fortified town was just too strong for the defenders to handle.

Sometimes mines or large tunnels were dug beneath fortifications and propped up with timber. Once enough material had been removed from beneath the structure the timbers would be set on fire, and everything above the tunnel would collapse or at least be seriously damaged. The people who carried out this work were known as sappers. The Muslims were experts at mining and using fire against fortifications, which was what forced the crusaders to build with stone rather than wood in the first place, though it made construction much more expensive.

The entranceway through the walls of the fortified crusader city of Caesarea on the Mediterranean coast. Often such entranceways could be fired into by archers from hidden openings, or incendiary materials could be dropped on attackers trapped there.

Another technique used by those besieging a castle or town involved the use of a siege tower built of wood that could be moved to various locations around the walls of the besieged building. In 1140, the crusaders were besieging the city of Banyas and they employed a tall siege tower there. The Templar of Tyre describes it thus:

Now for the first time the situation of the besieged became intolerable; they were driven to the last extremity, for it was impossible to devise any remedy against the downpour of stones and missiles that fell without intermission from the moveable tower. Moreover, there was no safe passage within the city for the sick and

pres en lan de grace ensuiat
m̄.cc.iiij.ix au temps de cel
lui roy de france en lan de son

The siege of Akkon during the Sixth Crusade from AD 1248 to 1254, from a thirteenth-century manuscript illumination

wounded, or where those who, still strong and vigorous and sacrificing themselves in the defense of others, could withdraw for rest after their labors.

Most of the time, however, siege towers were flimsy affairs that could be destroyed easily by incendiary devices dropped or thrown at them by the castle's defenders, and there are relatively few accounts of such towers being decisive in the conquest of castles or fortified towns.

Both these accounts concern fortified towns rather than isolated strong castles that might often be constructed in almost invincible positions. Clearly a wide range of methods could be employed when besieging a castle, but invariably these required a large army and took a long time, which allowed for other forces to come to the aid of those within the castle. The crusaders held their castles in the Holy Land for nearly 200 years. Only an enormous and sustained invasion was able to break their strength and force the crusaders to return home to western Europe.

The ruins of Belvoir Castle in modern Israel. It was built by the Knights Hospitaller in AD 1168, captured by Saladin in 1189, and finally destroyed in 1220.

The Castles Today

 any of the castles and other buildings constructed by the crusaders still exist today and can still be visited. They lie mostly within the boundaries of Israel, Palestine, Jordan, and Lebanon. Some of them are very impressive and still quite complete, whereas others have left only a trace to show that they were once there. Ever since the earliest days, there have been conflicts over the Holy Land and they continue to this day. As a result, some of these castles are not protected and preserved as they should be. In contrast, many castles in western Europe are protected and support a thriving tourist industry.

Perhaps the most spectacular of all the crusader castles that survive is the former castle of the Knights Hospitaller, Krak des Chevaliers. The castle was built on a vast scale and is a clear demonstration of the kind of wealth acquired by the military orders. The Hospitallers received charitable donations from wealthy Europeans who visited the Holy Land and who were impressed by the work of guardianship and care that the Hospitallers undertook in the area. Using money raised in this way and money raised from the local Muslim population, this enormous castle was constructed. Other indicators of the wealth spent in the building of this castle are the fine sculptured details on arches and capitals (the tops of columns).

The castle was built in hostile territory but on such a scale that it was almost invincible. When the Muslims would periodically invade the area, the knights would simply retreat into their gigantic fortress until the trouble had passed and then emerge to retake the area. This demonstrates just how powerful a castle could be in sustaining control of a population that has been conquered. Had Krak des Chevaliers not been built, the whole region would have fallen back into Muslim hands much sooner.

At its perimeter the castle is more than 320 feet wide and nearly 600 feet long, sitting on a long spur of a mountain high above the surrounding land. There is a moat, now dry, that was fed by an aqueduct, and all the towers and other buildings survive at least in part. There is an entrance tunnel to the building that has holes in the roof (known as murder holes) from which the occupants could fire upon anyone who had gotten inside the building.

Another large castle belonging to the Knights Hospitaller exists at Margat. It stands on a hill overlooking the Mediterranean Sea and, although not quite as large as Krak des Chevaliers, is on a similar scale. The stone used to build Margat was not as soft as that used elsewhere, so it was not possible to carve it into ornate leaves. But the castle does exude a rugged power that makes up for this. Hugh Kennedy, in his book *Crusader Castles*, describes how the layout of the castle forces anyone entering it to be completely exposed to attack from above, leaving attackers no chance of escape.

Another view of Margat Castle in Syria. It did not fall into Muslim hands until AD 1285, and the sultan who besieged it convinced the defenders to surrender rather than allow his army to destroy it.

Margat was one of the last major crusader castles to fall to the Muslims, in 1285, when the army of Sultan Qala'un besieged it. It featured a complete double set of concentric walls of great strength. The sultan's siege engines and catapults could not breach the walls, so he put his sappers to work digging a mine through solid rock all the way to the circular keep. But his admiration for the castle was too great to finish its destruction. Instead, he invited some of the defenders to come out and inspect the mine. The crusaders saw that their defenses would soon crumble, so they accepted an offer of safe passage out of the area and surrendered Margat to the Muslims.

The crusader castle at Saone, in Syria. As the position of the photographer indicates, the castle is surrounded by a very deep ditch.

The castle at Saone dates from the twelfth century and utilizes structures from an earlier period. The original building on the site was constructed by the Byzantines and comprised a fairly large castle fortress on top of a ridge. The local crusader lord set about improving and rebuilding this site, and in doing so he created a ditch on a vast scale in order to separate the ridge on which the castle stood from the surrounding land. The ditch is 90 feet deep, 60 feet wide, and 450 feet long. It was so wide that a single castle drawbridge could not span it, so the crusaders left an upright pillar of

A view from outside the walls of Krak des Chevaliers. It was controlled by the Knights Hospitaller.

rock extending upward from the floor of this ditch, which allowed them to have two drawbridges. Water cisterns were placed near the outer walls so that mines dug underneath those walls could be flooded. The scale of the engineering work here is remarkable and, like that at Krak des Chevaliers, is of a magnitude rarely seen anywhere in Europe.

An impressive site to visit is the Templars' fortified town of Tortosa. Tortosa is a coastal town and, typically for the Templars, was built on an important trade route. The town was encircled by a large wall punctuated by square

Another view of Krak des Chevaliers, perhaps the most impressive of crusader castles. The round towers are massive, and the walls reaching up to the keep are sloped.

towers, with the main fortress of the Templars situated to the northwest of the town. It appears that the Knights Templar held this town from around 1150 and that their gradual fortification of it began from that date. It featured a very strong castle and a surrounding wall with eleven towers. There was an inner wall with a moated ditch between the two walls and, as mentioned earlier, a section of the wall reaching an astonishing seventy-five feet in height. Tortosa is also remarkable for having a surviving crusader cathedral.

Throughout the Holy Land many castles survive to varying degrees—from the dramatic ruins of Chastel Pelerin right down to the ruined castle towers of the minor nobles. Much of the archaeological evidence for all kinds of structures built by the crusaders in the Holy Land still needs to be examined, surveyed, and recorded. With rare exceptions, this area is also the only place where large examples of the architecture of the monastic military orders still survive.

The castles of the crusaders are the physical evidence of a medieval holy war waged against the Muslims by the Christians of the West in their attempts to settle and control the Holy Land. Their efforts spanned nearly 200 years and left not just castles, but whole towns, churches, houses, and roads. Today these castles are stunning and impressive architectural wonders. It is hard to imagine what it must have been like to build huge castles such as Chastel Pelerin and Krak des Chevaliers. By studying them and exploring the time in which they were built, we can get insight into the way these incredible structures were used and perhaps reflect upon the motives of those who ordered that they be built.

There must have been quite an intense belief in Christianity for people to have traveled all the way to the Holy Land to recapture it for that religion. But there must also have been a strong belief in the minds of the crusaders that the journey was worthwhile financially. They knew that they might be forgiven for their sins by traveling out to fight, but they also wanted to benefit in material ways for their service. And benefit they did when the land was divided up between the lords and barons, who were given new titles and property that had been taken from the people who lived there. A lot of pain, grief, and suffering must have been felt by many involved on both sides during this time, but the crusaders at the time must have felt justified in their actions even if it is now generally considered that fighting for religion is wrong.

There have always been conflicts in the Middle East, and these continue unabated right up to the present day. The castles of the Holy Land are a symbol of a former time when the land was fought over, and they should be preserved as a reminder of those times and the loss of life and freedom that the castles represent.

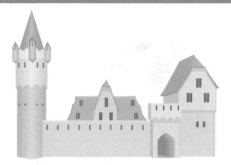

Glossary

aqueduct A channel used to transport water to cities in ancient times.

battlements The upper fortifications of castle walls, which might include crenellated walls and protruding towers.

Bible The book of writings sacred to Jewish and Christian worshipers.

crenellations The sawtooth-like openings along the upper walls of a castle.

crypt An underground tomb or chamber.

donjon A massive inner tower of a castle; another word for a keep.

enfilade To attack the flanks, or sides, of an enemy position.

foss Another term for a moat; a ditch filled with water.

gatehouse The stone entrance to a castle.

keep The central or inner tower or defensive structure of a castle.

military orders Charitable orders of monks with military training whose job was to protect Christian pilgrims.

mine   A tunnel built under the foundation of a castle that would be intentionally collapsed to bring down a portion of the castle wall or tower.

moat   A defensive, water-filled ditch, usually around the outer wall of a castle or fortified town.

monastery   A place of retreat, prayer, and work for those clerics who rejected the worldly life.

Muslim   A follower of Islam, the religion preached by the prophet Muhammad.

siege engines   Various wooden structures used to scale castle walls, to catapult stones against the walls, or to protect archers firing at the defenders.

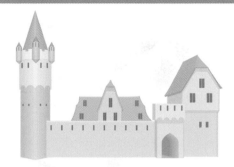

For More Information

Columbia University Medieval Guild
602 Philosophy Hall
Columbia University
New York, NY 10027
e-mail: cal36@columbia.edu
Web site: http://www.cc.columbia.edu/cu/medieval

Dante Society of America
Brandeis University
MS 024
P.O. Box 549110
Waltham, MA 02454-9110
e-mail: dsa@dantesociety.org
Web site: http://www.dantesociety.org/index.htm

International Courtly Literature Society
North American Branch
c/o Ms. Sara Sturm-Maddox
Department of French and Italian
University of Massachusetts at Amherst
Amherst, MA 01003
e-mail: ssmaddox@frital.umass.edu
Web site:http://www-dept.usm.edu/~engdept/icls/
    iclsnab.htm

Medieval Academy of America
1430 Massachusetts Avenue
Cambridge, MA 02138
(617) 491-1622
e-mail: speculum@medievalacademy.org
Web site: http://www.medievalacademy.org

Rocky Mountain Medieval and Renaissance Association
Department of English Language and Literature
University of Northern Iowa
Cedar Falls, IA 50614-0502
(319) 273-2089
e-mail: jesse.swan@uni.edu
Web site: http://www.uni.edu/~swan/rmmra/rocky.htm

Web Sites

Due to the changing nature of Internet links, the Rosen Publishing Group, Inc., has developed an online list of Web sites related to the subject of this book. This site is updated regularly. Please use this link to access the list:

http://www.rosenlinks.com/lma/crca

For Further Reading

Cartlidge, Cherese, *The Crusades: Failed Holy Wars.*
Detroit, MI: Gale Group, 1954.

Doherty, Katherine M., and Craig A. Doherty. *King Richard the Lionhearted and the Crusades in World History.* Springfield, NJ: Enslow Publishers, 2002.

Hallam, Elizabeth, ed. *Chronicles of the Crusades.* London: Weidenfeld and Nicholson Ltd., 1989.

Platt, Richard, and Melanie Rice. *Crusades: The Battle for Jerusalem.* New York: DK Publishing, 2001.

Bibliography

Allen-Brown, Reginald. *English Castles.* London: Batsford, 1954.

Armstrong, Karen. *Holy War: The Crusades and Their Impact on Today's World.* London: MacMillan Ltd., 1988.

Barber, Malcolm. *The New Knighthood: A History of the Order of the Temple.* Cambridge, UK: Cambridge University Press, 1994.

Billings, Malcolm. *The Cross and the Crescent.* London: BBC Publications, 1987.

Hallam, Elizabeth, ed. *Chronicles of the Crusades.* London: Weidenfeld and Nicholson Ltd., 1989.

Kennedy, Hugh. *Crusader Castles.* Cambridge, UK: Cambridge University Press, 1994.

Nicholson, Helen. *Templars, Hospitallers and Teutonic Knights: Images of the Military Orders 1128–1291.* Leicester, UK: Leicester University Press, 1995.

Riley-Smith, Jonathan, ed. *The Oxford Illustrated History of the Crusades.* Oxford, UK: Oxford University Press, 1995.

Robinson, John J. *Dungeon, Fire and Sword: The Knights Templar in the Crusades.* London: Michael O'Mara Books Ltd., 1991.

Seward, Desmond. *The Monks of War: The Military Religious Orders.* London: Penguin Books, 1995.

Index

About the Author

Brian Hoggard is an independent researcher with broad historical and archaeological interests. His current research focuses on beliefs in Britain in the sixteenth to eighteenth centuries. He has also completed a book all about a hill in Worcestershire called *Bredon Hill: A Guide to its Archaeology, History, Folklore and Villages*, which was first published in 1999 by Logaston Press. Brian plays guitar and also teaches guitar in schools and colleges within Worcestershire. He currently lives in the city of Worcester.

Photo Credits

Cover © Vistoars/AKG London; p. 4 © Sonia Halliday Photographs and Laura Lushington; pp. 7, 18, 34, 36, 39, 40 © AKG London; pp. 9, 44 © British Library/AKG London; pp. 11, 12 © Jane Taylor/Sonia Halliday Photographs; p. 15 © Jean-François Amelot/AKG London; pp. 21, 46 © Erich Lessing/AKG London; p. 51 © Tarek Camoisson/AKG London; pp. 22, 24, 25, 26, 30–31, 33, 43, 49, 50, 52 © David Halford.

Designer: Geri Fletcher; **Editor:** Jake Goldberg; **Photo Researcher:** Elizabeth Loving